Aloha- 11/14/94

To:
Bill & Coralie Smith
Congratulations on
your new ownership of
your Vacation Home
in Kauai -

The Lawai Beach Resort—
You can look forward
to many endless
Vacations in the
Beautiful Garden Island

Mahalo—

Dave Toomey

Niihau

Kauai

Oahu

Molokai

Maui

Lanai

Kahoolawe

Hawaii

Welcome to our beautiful Garden Island and thank you for supporting Wilcox Memorial Hospital! On behalf of Wilcox Memorial Hospital, the Wilcox Hospital Foundation is pleased to present to you *From the Skies of Paradise Kauai*. We, who are privileged to live on Kauai, do not often experience this island as you will in this lovely book. You will enjoy being able to take wing and to drift with the currents over this precious land that is our corner of paradise.

We, at Wilcox Memorial Hospital, have been serving the healthcare needs of the people of Kauai, residents and visitors alike, for over fifty years. We are proud of our aloha spirit and the high standard of patient care we have nurtured over the years. We believe that a caring touch creates a healing environment and that our contribution to the health of our community also enhances the quality of life on Kauai. We love this unique island and hope you will come to cherish it as we do.

Mahalo for caring!

David W. Pratt
Chairman

FROM THE SKIES OF PARADISE

KAUAI

Aerial Photography by Douglas Peebles

Text by Chris Cook

 Wilcox Memorial Hospital

 Grove Farm Company Incorporated

ABOUT OUR SPONSORS . . .

GROVE FARM PROPERTIES, INC.
GROVE FARM LAND CORP (KUKUI GROVE CENTER)
GROVE FARM ROCK COMPANY

Grove Farm Company, Incorporated was founded in 1864 by George N. Wilcox. Since that time, the family-owned company has expanded its original plantation operations into a multi-faceted corporation, whose various operation subsidiaries and divisions remain dedicated to providing Kauai and its people with a future in harmony with its rich heritage.

Copyright © 1991
  by Mutual Publishing
Photographs © by Douglas Peebles
Designed by Bechlen/Gonzalez, Inc.

1 2 3 4 5 6 7 8 9
First Edition October 1991

Printed in Korea
ISBN 0-935180-51-6

Mutual Publishing
2055 North King Street
Honolulu, Hawaii 96819
Telephone (808) 924-7732
Fax (808) 734-4094

CONTENTS

Kauai's majestic beauty is legendary, renowned among all of Hawaii's people. Ancient Hawaiian chants once sung before the kings of Kauai boast: "Kauai kilohana—Beautiful is Kauai beyond compare". These words still ring true today, for Kauai's 555 square miles encompass perhaps the most spectacular scenery found within one island in all of Polynesia.

Emerging from the depths of the Pacific long before Oahu and the main Hawaiian islands, Kauai is geologically the oldest of them all. Today the lush world of flora and fauna covering the eroding volcanoes and rich red soil plains of the island provide a canvas for a fantastic landscape painted with scenic drama, warm sunlight tones, lush tropical colors, and washed by passing tradewind showers.

Mount Waialeale, "The Wettest Spot on Earth" with an average rainfall of over 400 inches, looms above the island's coastal towns. Hundreds of waterfalls cascade down the interior mountains giving life to the verdant rain forests and plains of the "Garden Island." In contrast to Kauai's misty interior, dozens of sunny beaches and coral reefs ring the island.

The first people to arrive on Kauai's shores may have been the mythical, leprechaun-size Menehune. It is certain that a voyaging canoe from the Marquesas Islands brought Polynesians to Kauai about 1500 years ago.

Kauai's physical and cultural isolation from Oahu across the 72-mile-wide, 10,000-foot-deep Kauai Channel gained it a reputation as the "Separate Kingdom". This isolation ended on January 18, 1778, when Captain James Cook of Great Britain anchored off Waimea discovering Kauai as well as the Hawaiian Islands.

Politically, the isolation ceased in 1810 when Kaumualii, the last king of Kauai, deeded Kauai to Kamehameha the Great in a treaty aimed at saving the lives of Kauai's people. Sadly, the treaty ended generations of rule by Kauai-born *alii,* or chiefs, who were considered to possess the bluest blood of all Hawaii's rulers.

Hawaii's first New England missionaries established a base at Waimea in 1820. The island's schools, hospitals and many businesses were begun by descendants of these early spreaders of the Gospel.

The first commercial sugarcane plantation in Hawaii began operating in 1835 at Koloa. The intermarriage of sugar plantation workers from China, Japan, Portugal, the Philippines, Korea and other distant nations with the Hawaiian and western population created the multi-cultural society that peoples Kauai today.

Looking back to this colorful heritage, the people of Kauai desire to retain their rural lifestyle as the island's population grows. Zoning laws require that building be no higher than the top of a tall coconut tree.

This rural ambiance combined with Kauai's majestic scenery continues to draw artists and writers—as well as visitors—from across the world. Filmmakers rave about the island, selecting Kauai for most feature films shot in Hawaii.

Equally taken with Kauai is Hawaii-based photographer Douglas Peebles. In *From the Skies of Paradise Kauai* Peebles continues a photographic tradition, begun in the glass-plate era by Ray Jerome Baker, and later expanded upon by master photographers Ansel Adams and Robert Wenkam, of presenting Kauai as a unique environmental treasure.

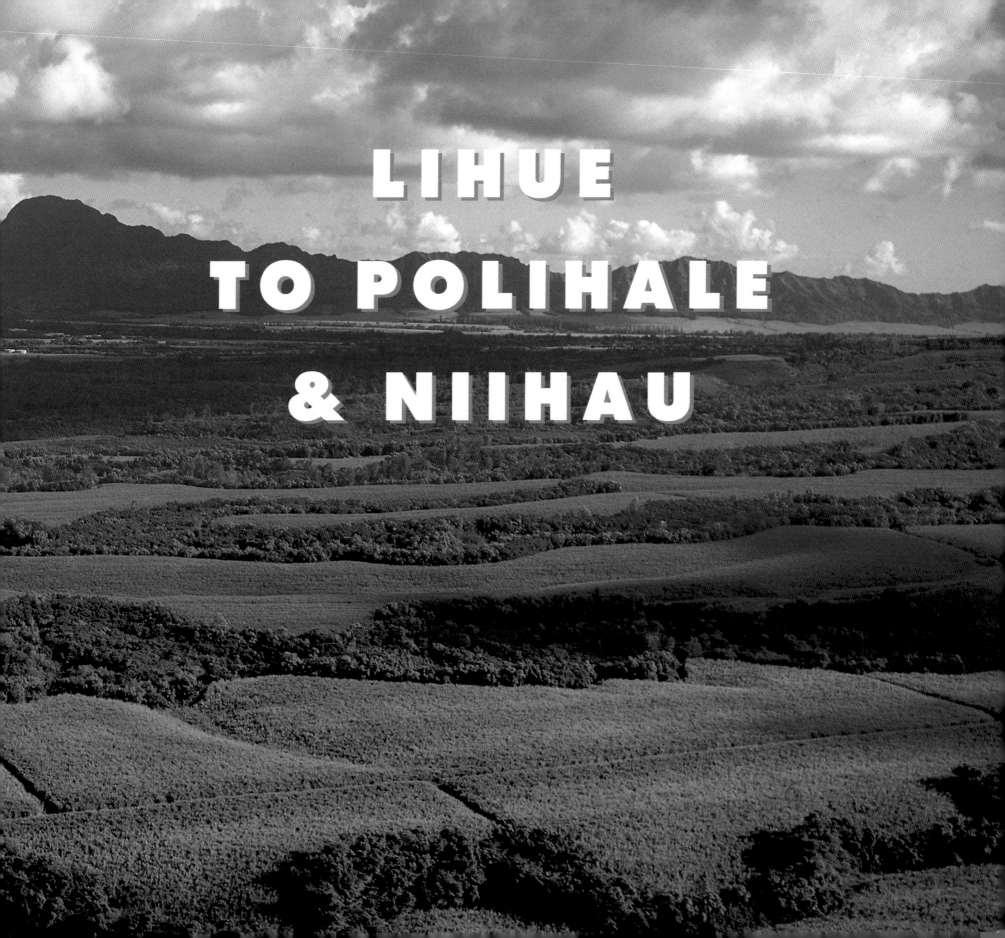

LIHUE
TO POLIHALE
& NIIHAU

From the bustling commercial and government center in Lihue on the east side, to the barren desert sands of Polihale where the Na Pali Coast begins and the west side ends, Kauai displays a separate face, distinct in mood, scenery and historical heritage.

A wondrous backdrop to the area is towering Waialeale and its sister peaks which stand inland, constant stark and majestic reminders to the area's residents and visitors that the Polynesian island's roots run deep in the land.

Down-to-earth Lihue is the hub of the island: the epicenter of air and sea transportation, seat of county government, the commercial and banking center of Kauai, and the starting point of both main highways. Set within verdant sugarcane fields that have been worked for over a hundred years and nearby world-class resorts, the tiny capital is poised at the crux of Kauai's future.

The town was begun by nineteenth-century missionary sons and daughters who were joined by British and European immigrants in establishing sugarcane plantations and commercial enterprises that stand today as island establishments. The legacy of G. N. Wilcox, the son of Waioli missionaries Abner and Lucy Wilcox, continues to serve the island through the G. N. Wilcox Memorial Hospital, the "living museum" at Grove Farm Homestead, the harbor at Nawiliwili and the many commercial holdings that have sprung from his Grove Farm plantation lands.

Over the Haupu range that looms south of Lihue life slows down and balmy sunny days are the norm. Isolated and unpopulated Kipukai is a "never-never land" set apart by topography from the charming stretch of

PREVIOUS PAGES: *The verdant sugarcane fields of Lihue Plantation and the Haupu Range border Lihue, Kauai's capital. The geometry of the fields is outlined by cane haul roads of red soil that radiate out from the plantation's mill in Lihue and stream beds covered in thick foliage which snake across the landscape.*

LEFT: *All roads lead to Lihue, Kauai's county seat. The island's center for banking, shipping, education, shopping and medical services, the bustling town is set upon a plateau overlooking Nawiliwili Harbor. Lihue's prominence dates back to the mid-1800s, when Kauai's Hawaiian Governor Kaikioewa began building there.*

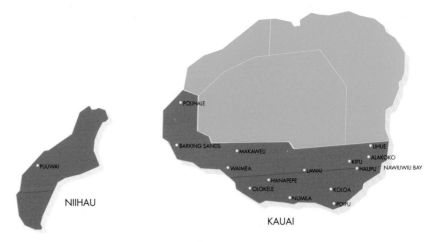

POLIHALE
BARKING SANDS
MAKAWELI
LIHUE
KIPU
ALAKOKO
PUUWAI
WAIMEA
LAWAI
HAUPU
NAWILIWILI BAY
HANAPEPE
OLOKELE
KOLOA
NUMILA
NIIHAU
POIPU

KAUAI

resort hotels, restaurants and shops along the coves, coral reefs and white sands at Poipu Beach. Upstream from Poipu, Koloa Town is the birthplace of Hawaii's sugar plantations with operations ongoing since 1835.

All of Kauai's sugarcane is milled at plantations in Lihue and towns to the south and west. Still in operation in the 1990s are Lihue Plantation, McBryde Sugar, Olokele Sugar and Gay & Robinson.

Graceful Lawai Valley, and the thousands of rare tropical plants thriving within the National Tropical Botanical Garden, are west of Koloa. Above the lush coastal valley is the rolling hill country surrounding Kalaheo, a rural town known for its Portuguese heritage.

Beyond Kalaheo the moist windward tradewind weather retreats, displaced by the arid, perennially warm clime of the sunny west side. In large agricultural tracts south of the town groves of macadamia nuts and coffee trees mark a transition away from sugar growing.

Life here is led somewhat apart from the mainstream in Lihue. Many west siders living in the coastal towns of Eleele, Hanapepe, Makaweli, Waimea, Kekaha and Mana rely on earnings from sugarcane plantation and resort work, fishing, and jobs at the Pacific Missile Range Facility north of Kekaha. All are proudly independent and consider the west side area a special place.

The spell of old Hawaii is still felt on the west side. Scenic panoramas of palm trees along sunny beaches dot the coast; Niihauans converse in Hawaiian in local grocery stores where crunchy local taro chips are sold; and churches dating back to the first New England missionary station established at Waimea in 1820 thrive.

Lihue Airport is the gateway to Kauai for inter-island and mainland jet flights. The island's mail, parcels and perishable Kauai-grown tropical flowers and fruits are sent to Honolulu, the mainland U.S. and internationally as cargo on the flights. Tour helicopters share the airport, transporting passengers over otherwise inaccessible terrain.

Lihue Plantation's mill grinds harvested sugarcane for export aboard ships docked at Nawili-wili. The cane is refined north of Oakland, California, and packaged by C & H Sugar. A by-product of the mill is electricity produced by steam-driven turbines that are powered by burning the pulpy bagasse remains of the milling process.

OPPOSITE: *Hanapepe Valley cuts south in the hill country near Kalaheo. Sugar is still king in the McBryde fields, but is now grown alongside coffee trees. Stands of macadamia nut trees and greenhouses protecting colorful tropical plants also point to attempts at diversifying the island's economy.*

PREVIOUS PAGES: *Islands inhabited by tropical birds and exotic animals at Kauai Lagoons, and the links of the championship Kiele Course, sit on a tableland above the Westin Kauai, Kalapaki Beach and Nawiliwili Harbor.*

OPPOSITE: *Cruise ships regularly visit Nawiliwili Harbor, docking alongside Matson Navigation Company's mainland container ships and Young Brothers' inter-island freight barges. Construction of the breakwater at the harbor entrance and the docks in the 1930s gave the island a modern port.*

Oceanfront golf holes, the elegant Inn on the Cliffs restaurant and the wedding chapel at Kauai Lagoons look out to Ninini Point and Nawiliwili Light Station. Below, Ninini Beach hugs the coast; snorkelers, swimmers, sunbathers and fishermen enjoy its isolation.

Fronting Kalapaki Beach is the luxurious Westin Kauai at Kauai Lagoons, a world-class resort destination that is a mecca for honeymooners, conventioneers and visitors from across the globe. Guests relax in one of Hawaii's largest swimming pools.

OPPOSITE: *Grove Farm Land Corporation's Kukui Grove Center is the island's main shopping center and built upon sugar lands once cultivated by pioneer sugar planter and missionary son G.N. Wilcox. Wilcox's simple but elegant estate is preserved intact at the Grove Farm Homestead Museum.*

PREVIOUS PAGES: *The Alekoko Fishpond along the Huleia Stream is known as the Menehune Fishpond after the diminutive race of people who, tradition says, built it in one night. Rather than mythical Hawaiian leprechauns, the menehune may have been a people of short stature who arrived earlier than Kauai's Polynesian settlers.*

Fragrant mokihana berries are found on the slopes of Mount Haupu, a peak thought by ancient Hawaiians to resemble their goddess Hina. Also known as the Hoary Head Mountains, the Haupu range is the dividing line between the verdant Lihue and Kawaihau districts and perennially sunny Poipu and Koloa.

OPPOSITE: *Kipukai is a picturesque coastal valley located between Nawiliwili and Mahaulepu. Inaccessible to the public by land, the valley is entered via a private road crossing the Haupu Range. Owned by the Waterhouse family, Kipukai retains a reputation as a remote fantasyland of breathtaking beauty.*

The fairways, greens and sand traps of the new Poipu Bay Resort Golf Course at the Hyatt Regency Kauai are located along the sunny south shore and mark the eastern end of the Poipu Beach resort. Nearby Mahaulepu apparently was once a well-populated Hawaiian fishing village.

26

OPPOSITE: *The grand Hyatt Regency Kauai at Shipwreck Beach is reminiscent of the romantic pre-World War II, art deco-influenced hotels of Waikiki. The ribs and keel of a wrecked ship lay at water's edge here for years until it disappeared in 1982 during the high surf and winds of Hurricane Iwa .*

Koloa's heritage as the birthplace of commercial sugar growing in Hawaii is symbolized by the steaming smokestack of McBryde Sugar Company's mill. Koloa Plantation opened in 1835, owned by a consortium of Yankee businessmen. The history of the area is preserved in restored buildings of Koloa town.

PREVIOUS PAGES: *Poipu Beach resort is known for its sparkling shore line of coves, white sand beaches, swaying palm trees, coral reefs and blue Pacific waters. The sunny weather and white sand beach annually draw thousands of guests to the fine resort hotels, vacation homes and condominiums within the resort.*

Lawai Kai is a coastal valley west of Koloa once owned by Queen Emma, the wife of Kamehameha IV. Today Lawai is synonymous with the 186-acre National Tropical Botanical Garden, where rare and endemic tropical plants flourish, as well as the landmark estate of its founder Robert Allerton and Queen Emma's simple cottage.

The Nomilu Fishpond at Palama Beach below Kalaheo is the most unusual fishpond in Hawaii. Supposedly, the natural salt-water lake becomes stirred up prior to volcanic eruptions on the island of Hawaii. According to Hawaiian mythology, the fishpond is situated within a volcanic cone dug by the goddess Pele.

PREVIOUS PAGES: *The head-quarters of McBryde Sugar Company is adjacent to their Numila Mill, or "new mill," along the back road from Kalaheo to Eleele. A village of plantation homes forms a delta inland of the mill. The plantation town of Wahiawa once thrived in the fields to the west.*

The commercial centers of the west side are Port Allen and Hanapepe. Kauai Electric generates electricity for the island from its main works near the docks at Port Allen. Quaint Hanapepe's old-Hawaii ambiance attracts art galleries to its main street.

OPPOSITE: *A typical west side panorama between Kekaha and Hanapepe: long white sand beaches, sunny skies, rich red soil, sugarcane fields, looming interior mountains and valleys. Thorny, introduced kiawe trees dominate coastal vegetation, and red soil runoff from cane fields muddies the Pacific.*

PREVIOUS PAGES: *Pakala Village is a tightly-knit Hawaiian community, home to many families with roots on Niihau. Offshore of the village is Pakala's, (or Infinities), a summer surfing site famous for its seemingly endless left slide.*

OPPOSITE: *Star-shaped Fort Elizabeth, "The Russian Fort", has guarded the mouth of the Waimea River since 1816. Circumnavigator Captain James Cook of the British Navy, Hawaii's western discoverer, was believed by Hawaiians at Waimea to be the god Lono. Cook first set foot on Hawaiian soil up the coast near Waimea Town in 1778.*

Gay & Robinson's Olokele sugar mill on the coast at Makaweli stands with its emerald green fields of sugar and community of workers. The mill was founded by the family of Eliza Sinclair, a Scot from New Zealand who purchased Niihau Island for $10,000 in gold in 1864.

41

Pacific Missile Range Facility at Barking Sands, north of Kekaha, is a high-tech Navy defense systems test site. Fishermen and surfers are allowed on base when tests aren't on. Early Kauai navigators braved the skies from a packed sand airstrip south of the base.

OPPOSITE: *The beach dunes on Kauai's west side produce a distinctive "bark" when walked on. The sound gave its name to the beach, which runs from the sea cliffs at Polihale to Kekaha, 15 miles to the south. The beach is one of the longest and widest in all Hawaii.*

Niihau—Hawaii's Forbidden Island—lies in the lee of Kauai, just 17 miles across the Kaulakahi Channel from Waimea. But, in reality it is a world away.

The famous circumnavigator Captain James Cook landed near Kamalino Beach on Niihau's southwest shore in 1778. The Niihauans were unable to supply Cook with freshwater for Niihau is desert-like as the island lies in the "rain shadow" of Kauai's tall mountains.

In 1864, the 72-square-mile island was purchased by the Sinclair and Gay family. The new owners paid Kamehameha IV $10,000 in gold for a desert isle covered with a rare layer of vegetation following unusually strong rains.

Preserving a fragile rural Hawaiian community on Niihau is important to the Robinson family, the descendants of the original owners. To protect the island, visits by outsiders to Niihau's main village of Puuwai, where Hawaiian is still the common language and taught in the schools, are limited to invited guests of the Robinsons.

Life on Niihau for its 200 or so residents is simple. No paved roads nor utility lines mark the island. Men work as *paniolos* herding cattle and making charcoal; the women raise their children, teach in the school and collect and string the famed Niihau shell leis. A trip to Kauai aboard a surplus Navy boat is an event.

Recently the door to the island opened a bit. Jet helicopter tours now allow outsiders to set foot on isolated parts of the once totally forbidden island. Time will tell if this last enclave of old rural Hawaii will remain as it is today.

OPPOSITE: *Kii Landing to the west of Kaunuopou Point is a safe landing spot even in high surf for the weekly Niihau supply boat. Local legends claim a row of wooden kii, or "tikis", representing Hawaiian men once saved the landing from attack by evil spirits.*

The steep sea cliffs of Lehua Island face nearby Niihau's northern tip. The northern face of the eroded volcanic tuff cone is an open-crescent bay. Only seabirds live on the desolate island. In winter months huge waves pound the island while schools of dolphins and migrating humpback whales swim by.

OPPOSITE: *Tiny Puuwai Village is the population center of Niihau. Its 200 mostly native Hawaiian residents speak Hawaiian as their first language. School children are taught in Hawaiian and English, and work on solar-powered computers. Most of the men are employed by Niihau Ranch.*

To families living in isolated homesteads on arid Niihau, thorny kiawe trees are valuable materials for charcoal making. Niihau women walk or ride bicycles to beaches rich in prized Niihau shells (the leis they string are highly prized throughout Hawaii).

Backlit by the sunset, Kaali Cliff and the uninhabited valleys of northeast Niihau present a romantic scene visible from the west side. Though just 17 miles across the Kaulakahi Channel, Niihau is kapu, *or taboo, to outsiders, and a world away from life on Kauai.*

NA PALI COAST

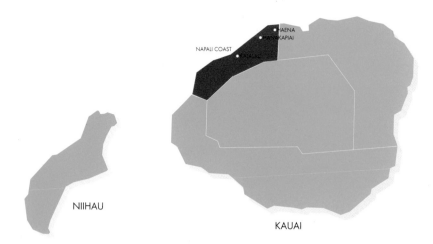

NAPALI COAST

HAENA
HANAKAPIAI
KALALAU

NIIHAU

KAUAI

Unfortunately, change has been wrought by introduced foreign animals and plants. Feral goats munching on ground cover have hastened cliffside erosion; cattle brought in to graze in the 1800s denuded native plants; and strange, exotic plants like sisal now grow alongside naupaka and other native endemic plants.

Thankfully, Na Pali is a wilderness area, a protected state park set apart from the mainstream of Kauai society, accessible only to the adventuresome. No roads cross into its lands.

Accounts of Na Pali are few, but insightful. Writers of Hawaiian myths, as well as Jack London who wrote of the exploits of freedom-loving Koolau the Leper's run from the law in Kalalau Valley, have found inspiration in its isolation and deep mystery. The seclusion and lure of Na Pali perhaps comes across best on the silver screen. In the valley behind the arch of Honopu a giant cinematic simian ruled in the 1976 remake of "King Kong", and millions of viewers have thrilled to a hang glider sweeping over the multi-hued pinnacles of Kalalau Valley in "To Fly", the feature film at the Smithsonian's popular aerospace museum.

Considered a golden asset in its untouched state, Na Pali is a place vital to the majesty of Kauai, as well as its soul.

OPPOSITE: *A geological wonder, Honopu Valley is still being cut from a massive volcanic dome by a steady stream of rainwater flowing down from the plateau of headwaters atop the island. Ancient trails down from Kokee to the coast once snaked along the walls of the valleys.*

Film makers ogle Na Pali's mysterious valleys, especially the hanging valley and arch of Honopu, which became Kong's Valley in the 1976 Hollywood remake of "King Kong". Summertime kayakers today land on a white sand beach where Hawaiian sailing canoes once transported valley dwellers along the coast.

OPPOSITE: *Spectacular huge winter surf blankets Na Pali's coast, washing out the wide sand beaches of summer and assaulting sea cliff faces. The cliff faces of Na Pali plunge steeply underwater for miles.*

PREVIOUS PAGES: *Rising skyward from Kalalau Beach is a natural cathedral, a fantastic display of Kauai's legendary scenery at its grandest.*

Tour boat passengers exploring Na Pali and sojourners in Kalalau Valley enjoy the solitude and majesty of the isolated wilderness area. Though inaccessible by motor vehicle, the adventuresome do explore Na Pali by foot along the Kalalau Trail, by sea aboard a kayak or boat and by air aboard touring helicopters.

OPPOSITE: *The goal of summertime campers who hike in along the 11-mile-long Kalalau Trail is the wide, white sand beach fronting Kalalau Valley. Beyond Kalalau, one must swim or boat in to enter the valleys. Helicopter landings are not allowed except in emergencies.*

OPPOSITE: *Cruise ship captains let their vessels drift slowly off Na Pali to allow passengers ample time to take in a superb, undisturbed view of the entire expanse. The passage along the deep valleys and towering sea cliffs is a highlight of cruises that circle the Hawaiian Islands.*

The Kalalau Trail climbs from coastal valleys to steep and narrow mountain trails beginning at the trailhead at Kee Beach. Days of blue skies, low surf and light winds are optimum for the trek, which lures hikers from around the world.

Salt spray of crashing winter swells on a calm day cloud Na Pali. Winter sea and weather conditions sometimes isolated for weeks the Hawaiians of the tiny villages that once existed in the valleys. Sailing canoes, swimming and trails along the coastal and inland were the only ways out.

OPPOSITE: *Hanakapiai Falls is the centerpiece of Na Pali's Hanakapiai Valley. The first valley in from Kee Beach, Hanakapiai is a popular wilderness area for day hikers. A trail runs two miles inland from Hanakapiai Beach to the base of the falls.*

Na Pali's pinnacles are mile-posts for hikers as well as veteran helicopter tour pilots. The fantastically-shaped peaks add to the mystique of Na Pali and lend an otherworldly air to the landscape.

Hawaiians once celebrated festive occasions by launching hau and papala wood firebrands from Mount Makana at Haena. Pits where the wood was stored and dried are still visible. Most know the peak as Bali Hai, the moody backdrop for the 1957 film production of the musical "South Pacific".

OPPOSITE: *Hook-shaped Makua reef runs from Haena Point to Haena Bay. A popular diving, windsurfing and surfing spot, it is known today as "Tunnels". Limahuli Valley stretches inland to the east of Mount Makana.*

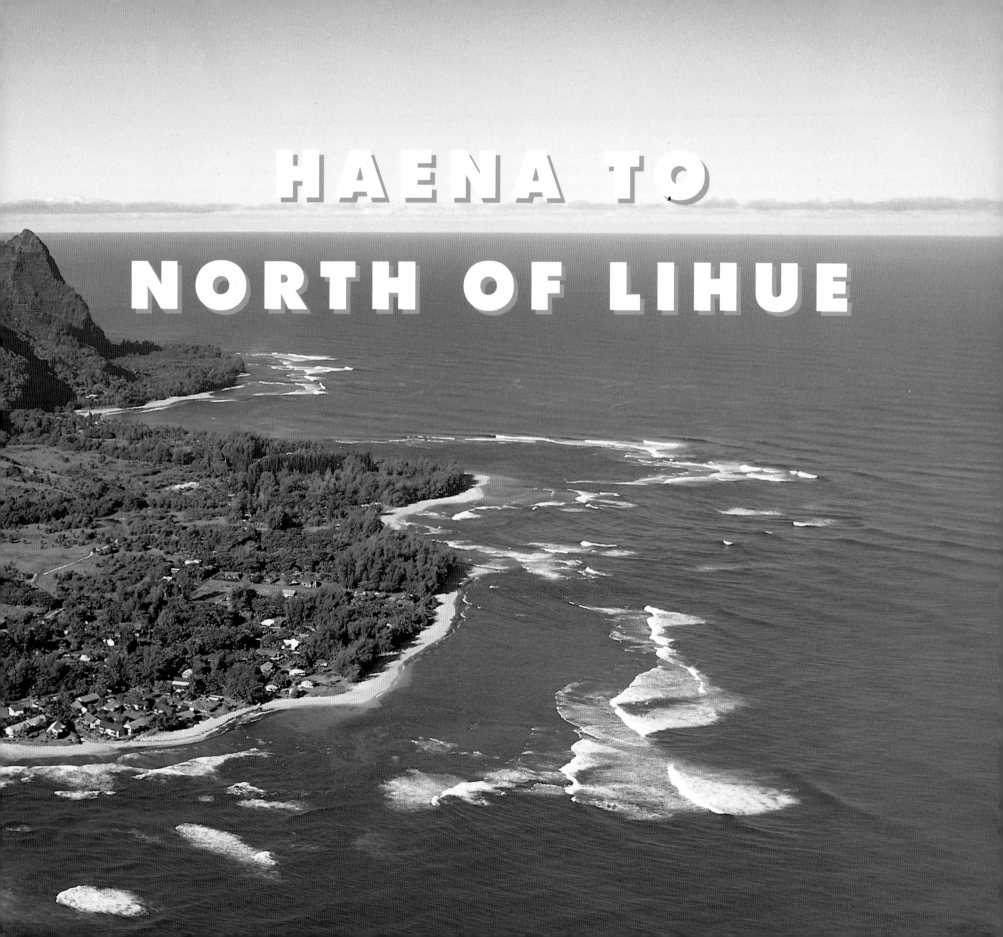

HAENA TO
NORTH OF LIHUE

Windward Kauai is rich in Hawaiian heritage and splendid scenic beauty from Haena Beach, the stopping place of the mythical volcano goddess Pele, to the twin falls of Wailua.

Encompassing the districts of Kawaihau and Hanalei, the area is growing in population while maintaining a lifestyle combining rural Hawaiian ways with the best of western living.

At the heart of Kauai's Hawaiian heritage is a complex of ancient rock-walled *heiaus,* or place of worship, along the Wailua River. The long and wide river is the only navigable one in Hawaii and popular for casual boat rides upriver to a natural amphitheater known as the Fern Grotto. Across the river is the Coco Palms Resort, a quaint South Pacific-style hotel with historic roots reaching back to the days of Deborah Kapule, Kauai's last queen.

Kapaa Town is the marketplace for the Kawaihau District. Its older plantation-style stores now do business next to boutiques, surfboard shops and a wide variety of eateries. The plantation flavor lingers in the town's architecture and aging landmarks like the Grant Wood-designed Roxy Theater.

Kealia, once a thriving sugarcane plantation community, is just past Kapaa. A weathered school house is all that remains of the James Makee Sugar Company.

Midway to Kilauea, the beginning of the island's north shore, is the Hawaiian lands and village of Anahola. The legendary circular "Hole in the Mountain" once tunneled through the jagged peaks that thrust up behind the town.

PREVIOUS PAGES: *Haena is a lush, tropical beach community rich in Hawaiian heritage and somewhat isolated from other north shore communities. To the east of Haena is Wainiha Valley where a nineteenth-century census numbered Menehune as residents. Homes of celebrities seeking quiet and isolation dot Haena and Wainiha.*

OPPOSITE: *Lumahai Beach is an exquisite uninhabited strand known for its pristine beauty and sea shell-rich tide-line. Some call Lumahai "The World's Most Beautiful Beach". Kahalahala, the east end, is the "Nurses Beach" of the 50s film "South Pacific".*

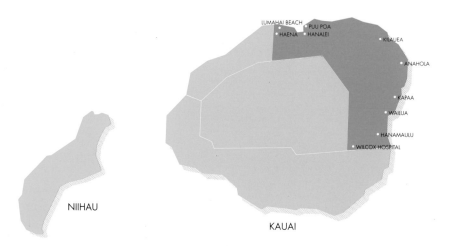

LUMAHAI BEACH
PUU POA
HAENA HANALEI
KILAUEA
ANAHOLA
KAPAA
WAILUA
HANAMAULU
WILCOX HOSPITAL

NIIHAU

KAUAI

The northern tip of Kauai is at Mokuaeae Island just below Kilauea Point. Atop the headland a lighthouse constructed in 1913 to guide Orient-bound ships still stands. The wildlife refuge at the point is home to thousands of seabirds including Laysan albatrosses and tropic birds.

Kilauea Town is a tight-knit, thriving community that beat all odds to recover from the closing of the Kilauea Sugar Mill in 1973. Now a guava plantation and valuable agricultural lots bordering the town promise a prosperous future.

Below Kilauea the Kalihiwai River meanders past groves of banana trees and a streaming waterfall, entering the Pacific along a small bay rich in Hawaiian legends.

At Anini Beach, families and picnickers enjoy swimming and fishing in a wide, calm lagoon along one of the longest barrier reefs in Hawaii.

Located on a tableland above the blue Pacific, elegant Princeville Resort looks across Hanalei Bay to Bali Hai, the mountain of South Pacific movie fame. Both locals and island visitors are lured to the resort by Princeville's 45 holes of golf, the most of any resort in Hawaii, and by the world-class Princeville Hotel.

Crossing the Hanalei Bridge below Princeville, one enters rural old Hawaii. Hanalei Valley boasts the largest taro patch in Hawaii, and a verdant, Gauguin-like landscape. Crescent-shaped Hanalei Bay is romantic by moonlight, and, by day, the delight of surfers and sunlovers.

Beyond Hanalei the lightly populated coastal valleys and white sand beaches of Lumahai, Wainiha, Limahuli, Haena and Kee still evoke the mystery and spirit of ancient Hawaii.

OPPOSITE: *The peaks of Hihimanu, Mamalahoa and Namolokama stand sentinel over crescent-shaped Hanalei Bay. The bay is rich in scenery, surf spots and history. Hanalei town is a laid-back community of beach homes, taro patches and low-key shops.*

74

Homes and visitor accommodations at Princeville feature panoramic views of ocean and mountains from a tableland 300 feet above the Pacific. Named in honor of Prince Albert, the son of Kamehameha IV, Princeville was founded in the 1860s as a plantation and retreat from the rigors of Honolulu.

OPPOSITE: *Princeville is internationally renowned for its championship golf courses. The new 18-hole Prince Course is already top-rated, and ranked the most difficult course in Hawaii; the 27-hole Makai Course features an unforgiving hole with a drive across a coastal chasm.*

OPPOSITE: *Anini Reef is one of the longest and widest fringing reefs in Hawaii. A quiet beachfront community, Anini comes alive on weekends with windsurfers, campers and polo at Anini Polo Field.*

For over 70 years, Kilauea Light guided ships past Kauai to and from the Orient. Today, Kilauea Point is a wildlife refuge, with the largest seabird colony in the main Hawaiian Islands. Lands acquired for the refuge above Kilauea crater offer nesting Laysan albatrosses and spectacular ocean views for visitors.

PREVIOUS PAGES: *Isolated beaches south of Anahola attract adventurous beachgoers and fishermen. At Anapalau Point footprints are rarely seen on beaches requiring access through sugarcane lands.*

A mostly Hawaiian community lives along the white sand beach and interior valley at Anahola Bay. A huge round hole through the nearby Anahola mountains was the source of Hawaiian legends.

OPPOSITE: *Kapaa, the main town of Kawaihau, the most populous Kauai district, is a former pineapple cannery and rice mill town, which now attracts boutiques, restaurants and businesses aimed at visitors to its main street of local-style stores.*

Wailua Beach, Lydgate Park's salt-water pool, comfortable resort hotels, and the Wailua River, the only navigable river in Hawaii, attract visitors and residents alike. Nonou Mountain, popularly known as the Sleeping Giant, provides a curious backdrop.

85

Once home to Hawaiian alii, *or chiefs, Wailua Homesteads is now a bedroom community set in the highlands above Wailua River and offers its residents breathtaking views of Mount Waialeale. Opaekaa Falls greets visitors, who pull off at a popular lookout.*

OPPOSITE: *The accommodations, activities, restaurants and shopping areas from Kapaa to the Wailua River are part of the Royal Coconut Coast. The area is named after groves of coconut trees once* kapu *to all but Hawaiian* alii.

OPPOSITE: *The twin falls of Wailua, north of Lihue, delight viewers who can drive to an overlook above the falls. Local lore says Hawaiian chiefs dove from the top of the eighty-foot cliffs to prove their courage.*

A cane haul truck rushes to mill along packed red dirt roads that wind through Lihue Plantation sugarcane fields mauka of Hanamaulu.

The Ahukini cutoff road leading to Lihue Airport bisects Hanamaulu Valley, an ancient Hawaiian land tract now home mostly to plantation workers and their families. Below, an overpass once crossed by narrow-gauge sugar trains recalls bygone days.

OPPOSITE: *Wilcox Memorial Hospital provides a wide range of modern medical services and a healing environment to Kauai's people. The hospital was founded in 1938. A new wing dedicated in 1990 is a source of community pride, as well as a boon to the hospital's health care services.*

WAIMEA CANYON & KOKEE

Kauai's interior lands are a remote, mysterious backdrop to the comings and goings of everyday life on the island; geological wonders viewed close-up only by hunters, hikers and helicopter sightseers who dare to venture in for brief stays.

Waimea Canyon, the "Grand Canyon of the Pacific", is a ten-mile-long slice of arid terrain reminiscent of its namesake that cuts inland of Kauai's west side. The 2000- to 3000-foot-high walls of the ever-eroding red, copper and green-blue serrated cliffs wind down from below the island's misty interior peaks to Waimea Town on the coast.

Geologists explain Waimea Canyon as one flank of the gigantic "dissected dome" built up by the great extinct volcano that formed most of the island ages ago. At the peak of this dome is the source of the waters that have formed the canyon.

In sharp contrast to bone-dry Waimea Canyon is Mount Waialeale, a tall peak with a dubious reputation as the wettest spot on earth. Almost constantly shrouded in misty clouds, Waialeale's plateau is a mysterious world of ferns and ohia lehua trees set in a cool, damp rain forest. Just south of Waialeale is its sister peak Kawaikini, the highest point on the island at 5,170 feet. Ancient Hawaiian poets who saw the rainwater running off the plateau as a sacred resource composed "The Water of Kane", the most poetic of all Hawaiian chants.

Absorbing a sizable amount of Waialeale's rainfall is the Alakai Swamp. Set in the remains of the largest extinct volcanic caldera to be found in the Hawaiian Islands, the Alakai is home to rare Hawaiian forest

PREVIOUS PAGES: *An uncountable number of waterfalls spilling down mysterious Waialeale Crater carry the waters of "The Wettest Spot on Earth" to windward Kauai. The signature cleft at the top of the crater marks the peak of Mount Waialeale.*

OPPOSITE: *Hidden waterfalls cascade into pools tucked away in the interior mountains. Rarely seen until helicopter tours of the island began, the pristine high country is home to rare Hawaiian plants and forest birds.*

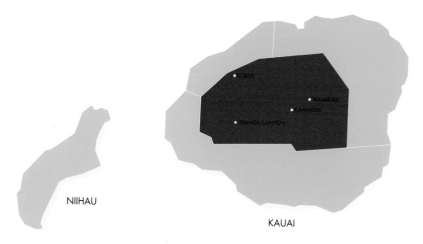

NIIHAU

KAUAI

birds, endangered native plants and dense thickets of tree ferns. Experienced hikers have disappeared into the swamp never to be seen again, perhaps disoriented by the low-lying fogs that often blanket the area.

At the southwest border of the Alakai the crisp, the highland forest of Kokee State Park begins. About ten degrees cooler than the environment 4,000 feet below at sea level, Kokee is laced with forty-five miles of hiking and hunting trails. Centuries ago tall koa logs were felled for Hawaiian sailing canoes in Kokee's forest, and the woodland was considered to be a home to the gods.

Today, Kokee's 4,345 acres retain their native lure. Visitors can see stands of stately koa trees; mountain streams stocked in season with trout; rare Hawaiian forest birds; wild moa, or Tahitian chickens, whose ancestors came with early Polynesian settlers; and a number of lookouts offering majestic views of the uninhabited valleys of Na Pali. Unusual endemic Hawaiian plants, including the iliahu, a palm-like plant related to the famous silversword found at Maui's Haleakala crater, thrive along an easily accessible nature walk.

Fragrant mokihana berries grow on a low bush in the Kokee uplands. Highly prized leis strung of mokihana are treasured by Kauaians, who years ago chose the plant over native flowers as Kauai's symbol.

Information, lodging and food are available at the park's center at Kokee Lodge, and the story of man and nature at Kokee is on display at the nearby Kokee Natural History Museum. Cabins with fireplaces are booked at the lodge. The rustic hideaways are very popular, and must be secured months in advance.

OPPOSITE: The plateau atop the dormant volcano that formed most of Kauai is the eroded surface of the largest volcanic caldera ever formed in the Hawaiian Islands.

At 5,170 feet, Kawaikini is Kauai's tallest mountain peak. Usually shrouded in mist, the peak is especially visible during periods of dry kona weather. The place name was translated by noted Hawaiian legend writer William Hyde Rice as "water-in-multitudes".

OPPOSITE: *Dwarf foliage and harsh weather at Kauai's upper peaks present a striking contrast to the island's balmy coastal environment. Hawaiian plants, which flourish in the fragile environment, draw botanists in search of unnamed species.*

98

PREVIOUS PAGES: *Pilgrimages up jagged windward ridges to a sacred* heiau, *or place of worship, at Waialeale were made by Hawaiians in earlier days. Waialeale translates as "rippling water", and refers to the pond atop the peak. Legends say a spring at the summit casts up beach sand and seashells.*

Tradewind-borne cumulus clouds gather above Kauai's highest mountains, again drawing a curtain of mystery over the island's interior.

OPPOSITE: *Waialeale peeks from behind a curtain of white clouds. Tour helicopters enter Waialeale crater to give passengers an unforgettable close-up view of cascading waterfalls hundreds of feet tall.*

102

Endless glorious and dramatic moods shade the pristine verdant landscape at Waialeale.

OPPOSITE: *A passing glimpse of stunning cloud-shrouded cliff faces highlighted by sun rays breaking through the mist remains forever in one's treasured memories of Kauai.*

PREVIOUS PAGES: *The multi-hued cliffs of Waimea Canyon, the "Grand Canyon of the Pacific", provide an ever-changing pattern of earthtone colors in sun and shadow. Eons of geological time recorded by stream waters and wind are visible in the multi-layered cliff faces, providing information to scientists and a sense of wonder to spectators.*

OPPOSITE: *Weathered, other-worldly serrated ridgelines are the backbone of Kauai's mountains. Inhabited only by wild boars and feral goats, these badlands are alien and distant from the everyday life of the island.*

Distinct contrasts of terrain, vegetation and coloring highlight the many chapters of geological history visible in the cliffs of Waimea Canyon. Evidence of recent massive landslides hints at the sudden changes the terrain may take.

NASA's sole Hawaii tracking station once guided astronauts in orbit high above the central Pacific. Located at Kokee, the station is now a backup to a satellite-borne, high-tech tracking system.

OPPOSITE: *Visitors at Kalalau Lookout at Kokee drive up and peer 3,000 feet down to Na Pali's Kalalau Valley. A series of hiking trails at Kokee offers equally spectacular views of other Na Pali valleys.*

FOLLOWING PAGES: *The source of the Hanalei River is deep within a watershed below Waialeale. The river flows for miles downstream into Hanalei Valley providing irrigation for the largest patch of taro in Hawaii at Hanalei.*

ABOUT THE PHOTOGRAPHY

Kauai is the most beautiful of the islands from the air. I have been doing aerial photography of Hawaii for about 15 years and I never tire of flying over Kauai. On a sunny day the blues and greens are dazzling and Waimea Canyon has a palette of colors that I never see elsewhere. On a rainy day, Kauai's colors are softer than seen on the other islands but as you fly around there are more waterfalls than you can possibly count. This is especially true of Waialeale crater and Hanálei valley. It is stunning.

I did all the photos in this book from helicopters. The most important part of aerial photography is finding pilots to work with. I had the help of many and want to thank: Gardener Brown of Ohana Helicopters, Chuck di Piazza of Air Kauai, and the pilots from Kenai Helicopters, South Sea Helicopters and Island Helicopters. I also especially want to thank H. D. "Woody" Wood and Robert Stanga of Makani Kai Helicopters for flying me over from Oahu in their Robinson 22.

Of secondary importance is the equipment. Most of the photography was done with a Pentax 67 medium format camera and a gyroscope. The lenses were 45mm, 55mm, 75mm, and 135mm.

Douglas Peebles

Photography by Douglas Peebles
Produced by Bennett Hymer
Text by Chris Cook
Corporate Liaison:
    Galyn Wong

Art Direction and Design by
    Fred Bechlen and
    Leo Gonzalez
Design Assistant:
    Lilia Chua
Maps: Christine Wilhite /
    Time2Design

Typeset by Typehouse Hawaii
Headlines: Futura Extra Black
Text: Baskerville Roman
Captions: Baskerville Italic

Printed and Bound in Korea